The Leaves Fall All Around

■SCHOLASTIC

Children's Press®
A Division of Scholastic Inc.
New York Toronto London Auckland Sydney Mexico City
New Delhi Hong Kong Danbury, Connecticut

Early Childhood Consultants:

Ellen Booth Church
Diane Ohanesian

© 2010 Scholastic Inc.

1 2 3 4 5 6 7 8 9 10 R 19 18 17 16 15 14 13 12 11 10   62

Library of Congress Cataloging-in-Publication Data

Mack, Steve, 1976–
   The leaves fall all around / Steve Mack.
      p. cm. - (Rookie preschool)
   ISBN-13: 978-0-531-24402-9 (lib. bdg)   978-0-531-24577-4 (pbk.)
   ISBN-10: -0-531-24402-4 (lib. bdg)   0-531-24577-2 (pbk.)

 1. Leaves - Juvenile literature. 2. Leaves - Color - Juvenile literature.
 3.   Fall Foliage - Juvenile literature. I. Title. II. Series.

   QK649.M25 2009
   508.2 - dc22   2009004776

There was a tree.

And, oh that tree,
was the prettiest tree
that you ever did see.

3

The green leaves grew all around, all around.

4

The green leaves grew all around.

5

And on that tree, the leaves turned gold,

the brightest gold that you ever did see.

The leaves turned gold
all around, all around.
The leaves turned gold all around.

And behind that tree, a cornfield grew,

8

the tallest corn that you ever did see.

And the tall corn grew
all around, all around.
The tall corn grew all around.

And near that tree, some pumpkins grew,

the biggest pumpkins that you ever did see.

The pumpkins grew
all around, all around.
The pumpkins grew all around.

11

And in that tree, looking for nuts,

were the hungriest squirrels that you ever did see.

The hungry squirrels
ran all around, all around.
The hungry squirrels ran all around.

And then the wind, blew windy and cold, the windiest wind that you ever did feel.

15

So, the gold leaves blew all around, all around.

The gold leaves blew all around.

Then on that tree, some snowflakes fell, the whitest flakes that you ever did see.

19

20

And the snowflakes fell all around,

all around.

And the snowflakes
fell all around.

23

Rookie Storytime Tips

This version of *The Leaves Fall All Around*, a favorite preschool song, celebrates seasonal changes. Talk about these changes while sharing this book with your child. It's a great way to build your child's observation, vocabulary, counting, and comprehension skills.

Invite your child to go back through the book and look for these signs of the seasons. It's a fun way to build his or her visual discrimination skills.

Pumpkins:
How many grew on the ground?

Leaves:
What colors are they? Why did they fall to the ground?

Squirrels:
Why were they in that tree?

Tree:
How did it change?

What other seasonal changes do you see in the book?